THE ESCAPISM OF OPERATIONS RESEARCH

THE ESCAPISM OF OPERATIONS RESEARCH

Niels Warrer

AARHUS UNIVERSITY PRESS

Printed on acid-free paper by Special-trykkeriet Viborg a-s
ISBN 87 7288 402 9

AARHUS UNIVERSITY PRESS
Building 170, Aarhus University
DK-8000 Aarhus C, Denmark

Published with financial support from the
Aarhus University Research Foundation

Contents

CHAPTER 1

Subject and Intention

This book is on those quantitative methods classified under the name of OR/MS, Operations Research/Management Science. The aim is to seek an explanation for the very modest empirical stand, which this discipline seems to have achieved.

The feeling of empirical weakness is probably widespread, and the explanations usually offered—to be accounted for later—seem to focus on Public Relations, on style, image, and attitude. Considering the age of OR/MS however, it might soon be worthwhile to look at the contents of the discipline itself in order to investigate, whether more tangible defects could cause lack of applicability.

The essence of the explanation found is lack of alertness to the realities of business, especially to time, trade and logistics. Confronted to these, the compatibility of concepts seems to stagger, the ability to cope with the tasks of industry vanishes, and even the intrinsic ideology becomes questionable.

The justification for such postulates is to be found in a closer investigation of selected, but recent and predominant OR/MS texts, the main characteristics and realism of which are evaluated by confrontation to industrial realities as they can be testified by ordinary official statistics.

Chapter 2 specifies the subject of the manuscript, OR/MS, by calling attention to the contents of recognized books, periodicals and congress papers. Interest is on the industrial scene alone, in accordance with the bulk of OR/MS texts. The chapter briefly reviews the information available on the empirical stand and supplies the main point of explanations offered by others.

Chapter 3 will specify and substantiate the detachments of reality to be found in OR/MS, the method of investigation to be outlined in the first section. The main interest is on time, trade and logistics, where those aspects of reality focused on in this manuscript are specified in section 2. The remaining sections are on OR/MS characteristics, to be documented in a three-step procedure. The section on Formulae will—by inspection of recent textbooks—select central typical expressions of the discipline. In these, the detachments of reality are identified: Scope, levels, cost and time, to appear explicitly in section 4. The characteristics found in textbooks are finally checked against papers from a recent high level conference on 'Multi-Stage Production Planning and Inventory Control'. Chapter 3 contributes those aspects of reality and literature to be referred to in the next chapter.

Chapter 4 is explanatory in order to outline why OR/MS achieved so modest empirical results in industry, the main points already mentioned above: Serious problems as to compatibility, competence and consistency.

Chapter 5 terminates by evaluation of the procedure followed and estimates the odds of OR/MS according to the conclusions drawn.

CHAPTER 2

Operations Research/Management Science

The discipline

Definition seems an indispensable opening statement for discussion on any chosen professional subject. The risk of objections seems equally unavoidable, agreement on the meaning of words traditionally difficult to obtain in academic circles. Professor Eilon (p. 5) wrote about that dilemma as regards OR/MS concluding that it is hardly worthwhile attempting comprehensive studies for an answer of general validity. However, a choice has to be made, and I have decided on a method that is explicit, operational and relevant to the intentions of this manuscript.

OR/MS presents itself as the contents of those textbooks, periodicals and conference papers to be specified below; I pretend no formal generality.

My choice is on four textbooks by Hax & Candea, by Silver & Peterson, by Johnson & Montgomery, and by Elwood S. Buffa, all well known to those familiar with the subject.

As to conference papers, my choice is the Mannheim Workshop on 'Multi-Stage Production Planning and Inventory Control' reported in the Springer-Verlag edition No. 266 of *Lecture Notes in Economics and Mathematical Systems*.

'Interfaces', especially the current 'Application Review' covering no less than 17 journals, is chosen to represent the periodical side.

That choice is as subjective as anyone, but defendable according to the aim of this survey from the following points of view:

The predominant textbooks specify the contents of a discipline to the common educational market, to the majority of business trainees. The concepts and methods thus lectured constitute the fundamental knowledge of the discipline for those entering the jobs of business. By these means, the bulk of educational effort in the discipline is delivered, hopefully to be justified by later practical application. If the contents of the subject come close to problems met afterwards, the chances for application improve. If not, the risk for waste is immanent. Textbooks are most relevant to the explanation looked for.

Still they are often considered lagging behind the scientific development and in order to counter objection of this character, their contents—as to those aspects of the discipline focused on—are checked against recent developments, conferences and periodicals.

The 1985 workshop of Mannheim by the European Working Group of Production and Inventory Control substantiates the conference side; no less than 40 specialists from 14 nations, among them well-known participants in the professional debate, attended the congress, which presents itself as one of the main activities in the production field in Europe.

'Interfaces' probably needs no introduction and the 17 periodicals mentioned will be listed below.

Evidently, I refrain from a literary detective-wise investigation in order possibly to find lesser-known OR/MS texts that might be less vulnerable to the postulates of this manuscript. Lesser known texts neither harm nor benefit very much. For explanation of empirical failure predominans and recognition are essential criteria for choice. The actual selection performed could easily be supplemented, but will hopefully be found relevant.

OR/MS comprises four main subjects as shown in *table 1* where, by reference to the number of pages found, the relative weight is illustrated. The naming of subjects comes very close to those of the book chapters classified.

Table 1. The subjects of OR/MS, measured by number of pages in four textbooks

Subject	Silver	Hax	Johns	Buffa	Total
Forecast	77	34	95	45	251
Inventory	353	97	89	39	578
Operations	-	135	77	109	321
Aggregate	129	128	217	103	577
Other*	143	96	34	370	643
Total	702	490	512	666	2,370

* Introduction, Evaluation, Strategic Planning, Appendices, Miscellaneous.

The subjects are conceptually well coordinated—to be shown later on. Forecasting methods furnish sales figures for aggregate planning, whose main task is to balance production and inventories so as to meet trend and season

in demand. Inventory and operational models handle remaining random fluctuations and decide on appropriate lot-sizing in production.

The same weighting of subject appear in the conference papers from
Mannheim as they are grouped and named by the editorial committee

Table 2. Mannheim papers (p. v)

Inventory-production and distribution systems	99 pages
Multi-stage lot-sizing	72 pages
Practical applications and hierarchical integration problems	78 pages
	—————
Total, 11 papers	249 pages

I shall be more accurate as to the sections and characteristics of the literature focused on later in the report. The aim so far is to be specific on the
source texts to be representatives of OR/MS.

Empirical shape

Ackoff, in his famous: 'The future of OR is past', in 1979 addressed the profession vividly enough to arouse real interest. He declared a criterion of suc-
cess, which so far seemed to have been neglected: The amount of practical
application. He found the empirical stand to be rather low and constantly
declining.

This view is repeated in Eilon's 1985-book: 'Management Assertions &
Aversions'. In Eilon's opinion (p. 41) OR is 'in crisis' mainly due to a still
more pressing lack of practical application.

Such opinions reappear occasionally in periodicals, e.g. 'MS/OR: A mid-
life crisis' by G.L. Lilien in Interface 1987 (2). The criterion of application is
a stubborn one.

However, investigations on application are rare and neither Ackoff nor
Eilon offered much evidence to support their views.

Still, some can be provided, and four will be reported on: Two company
surveys from 1986 and two investigations of the contents of periodicals 1983
and 1984-85-86 respectively.

Eiselt et al. in 1986 (Infor, vol. 24) reported on a survey in no less than
1000 Canadian companies. They also recalled previously published surveys

of application—either too old, unfortunately, or non-industrial. The 1,000 Canadian companies, seriously sampled but not delimitated to industry, received a questionnaire on the application of OR/MS. 328 replies were obtained, of which 227 indicated that no mathematical modelling was done at all. That leaves 101 firms to fill in the questionnaire and move ahead for further investigation (p. 290). In 61 of the firms no OR department existed, leaving a remainder of 39 companies with observable staff, the average personnel reported to be 5.7 persons. The survey investigates the character of projects in such a way as to measure the frequency of application: Annual use of the developed systems seemed to prevail.

Interpretation of statistics is a subjective matter of course, but the ordinary observer would probably find the empirical score to be poor.

Hogue and Watson in 1986 contributed a survey of 18 companies to Spraque's book on 'Current Practices in the Development of Decision Support Systems'. The found that in 89 percent of the companies, the OR/MS group had played no role at all in development of Decision Support Systems (p. 82) and that OR/MS personnel accounted for 5.6 percent of developmental resources in developing DSS (p. 83).

The information of these two surveys, the only ones found, can hardly be called contradictory.

Prevalence of reference in periodicals could possibly indicate the amount of practical occurence, silence to be taken accordingly as a sign of no application.

G. Lockett has reported on the 'Application of Mathematical Programming' (Management Science 1985.8). Of 200 Operations Research articles written in 1983, he found less than 3 percent to deal with real-world applications.

Table 3. Source periodicals, the Interfaces ms/or application review

Decision Sciences	Operations Research
MIS Quarterly	Journal of Marketing Research
Management Science	Socio-Economic Planning Sciences
Policy Science	Regional Science and Urban Economics
Urban Studies	European Journal of Operational Research
Growth and Change	Naval Research Logistics
Policy Science	Computers and Operations Research
Marketing Science	Journal of the Operational Research Society
Journal of Marketing	

In Interfaces, a panel of 4-5 experts investigates the current editions of the 17 periodicals listed in *table 3*; they search especially for articles on practical application among the aggregate volume.

Short abstracts are given of the articles selected, and the total number of 97 abstracts in the 1984-85-86 volumes have been further investigated for use in this manuscript. I have looked especially for application in industrial planning, the subject of OR/MS textbooks. The result is shown in *table 4*.

Table 4. Interfaces, applications review

Topics of abstracts	1984	1985	1986	Total
1. Public sector	15	21	12	48
2. Marketing projects	8	14	4	26
3. Industry planning	1			1
4. Miscellaneous	6	10	6	22
Total number of articles	30	45	22	97

1: Education, Defence, Community, Prisons, Hospitals, Traffic
2: Market test to answer project questions
3: The field of OR/MS texts
4: Mainly surveys, racetrack betting, insurance, agriculture, airlines - one article each, or not application anyhow.

Of 97 applications to be reported of in 3 years volumes of 17 periodicals only 1, one, was on the industrial field. The bulk was on the public sector, marketing projects or miscellanous. The editorial committee seems liberal as to the criterion of application, it should be pointed out. The one I have classified as industry names as follows: 'Formulation and solution of non-linear integer production planning problems for flexible manufacturing system' (Interfaces 84.1, p. 167). No practical application is reported of, but the problems selected are from an existing manufacturing system!

To terminate on the empirical stand: It is very difficult to question the opinions expressed by Ackoff and Eilon. Application seems out of consonance to the considerable amount of academic texts steadily being forwarded in industrial vocabulary.

Explanations offered

The intention of this study is to seek explanations for this weak empirical stand. Why OR/MS, in spite of this, proves so attractive to intellectuals and still supports a number of periodicals, could be the aim of a separate investigation.

The critics of OR/MS, Ackoff and Eilon, supplied explanations which will be shortly reviewed. Their opinion may be correct, but it is general in nature, not very specific. The writers, in spite of their expertise in the field—or maybe exactly for that reason—do not call specific OR formulae for trial and do not show specific OR statements to support their actual accusations—some loyalty might still have its effect. They do not, in my opinion, go to the bone of the subject. Recall for comparison the analysis of Orlicky on the use of inventory models in the field of dependent timephased demand (pp. 22)! The main statement of Ackoff is probably that

> OR came to be identified with the use of mathematical models and algoritms rather than with the ability to formulate management problems, solve them, and implement and maintain their solution in turbulent environment (p. 94).

OR was not aware of important implications of the changing environment, called upon by Ackoff be means of such concepts as reductionism, machinage, system-age, expansionism, and even aesthetics. In spite of the comments on the OR-difficulty in coping with uncertainty and in spite of the awareness of the OR phlegm to non-cybernetic controls Ackoff is rather paradigmatic in his attitude to the profession, not specific in pointing out, what exactly is wrong in the models and algorithms proposed.

Ackoff's article from 1979 aroused resentment among the fans for some time, but the perpetuum mobile of intrinsic academic texts grinds along that safe road of mathematics, which Ackoff so unambigously did renounce.

Samuel Eilon made the next larger effort for the principle of empirism in his 1985 book, in which especially chapters 2 and 3 are on OR/MS. His opinion of a low empirical stand has previously been stated, the chapters concentrating on explaining. Eilon selects nine sets of concepts found unclarified in OR/MS, causing difficulties in application. Some are on the modes of expression to be applied: Robustness, complexity, optimizing and satisfaction. One is tactical vs. strategic planning and the rest rather scattered:

Ethics, charging, organization being the main points. Concepts prevail and no specific OR/MS subject is identified. In the next chapter another line of reasoning is pursued: The weak empirical stand of OR/MS could be explained by the low organizational level, which members of the trade are presumed to have gained. Eilon might mingle cause and effect here: The reason for the level could be results achieved, not the other way round. The attitude of organizations, according to Eilon, is not favourable and an organizational debate on competition, dispersion, fragmentation, relegation and isolation is called for, if application has to be improved!

As can be seen, the explanations of Ackoff and Eilon are far from a tangible inspection of the contents of OR/MS doctrines as such. Faith in the 'right' application, whatever that may be, is never really shaken even if the disciples did not so far made things work.

Few people had attempted from outside the profession, to challenge OR/MS on its own ground and to explain the lack of applicability by reference to the properties of the application field. An exception is Orlicky, who in his book on MRP actually pulled the carpet from under much OR/MS modelling.

His distinction between independent and dependent demand is recalled and the explanation of the reasons why common inventory- and lot-sizing models cannot manage timephased industrial production will be referred to later on. Orlicky's mission was to promote the MRP system, and he did not engage OR/MS to a degree more than needed for that purpose. Above all, market relations and aggregate planning remained out of sight. The intention of this manuscript is different, the aim being to explain the empirical failure of OR/MS. As previously stated the full appearance would have to be engaged for such a purpose but at some points the analysis of Orlicky fully satisfies the intentions and will be recalled when needed. His method of explanation, confrontation of specific models to industrial conditions appears far more plain and efficient than the more general attitude of Ackoff and Eilon.

I shall try to proceed along that line by calling attention to some points, where OR/MS seems to evade realities and as a result, probably application as well.

Detachments from Reality

Investigation

The role of chapter 3 is to supply and specify those aspects and components of reality and literature focused at in the explanation to follow in chapter 4. Observations are separated from explanation in a desire to be precise on the demarcation line between objectivity and subjectivity.

The main viewpoint applied is, that if the formulae of OR/MS either neglect essential business realities or apply such delimitations in procedure that it is difficult to spot opportunities for application—if such is the case, it is understandable that the empirical stand will be low. If literature is detached from reality, its methods cannot deserve much attention—in the long run at least.

Explanation will need, as a consequence, specification of those aspects of realities and of literature to be focused on.

As to realities, nobody can claim to map in any absolute or total sense. Any text must put forward those aspects found relevant, and the justification for stating that such is the world. A pure reference to self-evident and common knowledge is quite usual in analytical economics, but a more solid foundation for the claim is preferable. Official, freely available statistics on Danish industry are drawn upon, not sophisticated at all, but plain facts on time and trade in business. They will appear in section 3.2.

The substance of literature has been selected already, and the closer look is to be accomplished as follows: Selected central textbook formulae are investigated thoroughly in order to extract precise specification of characteristics in objective functions and constraints. What exactly do they pronounce on business, what exactly is their conception of planning and coordination? Such specification is needed for explicit appointment of the detachments to be focused on, the subject of section 3.4. Having decided in that way what to look for, the chapter terminates the inspection of literature by observations in congress papers.

Figure 1. Logistic and chronological shape of operations and stocks

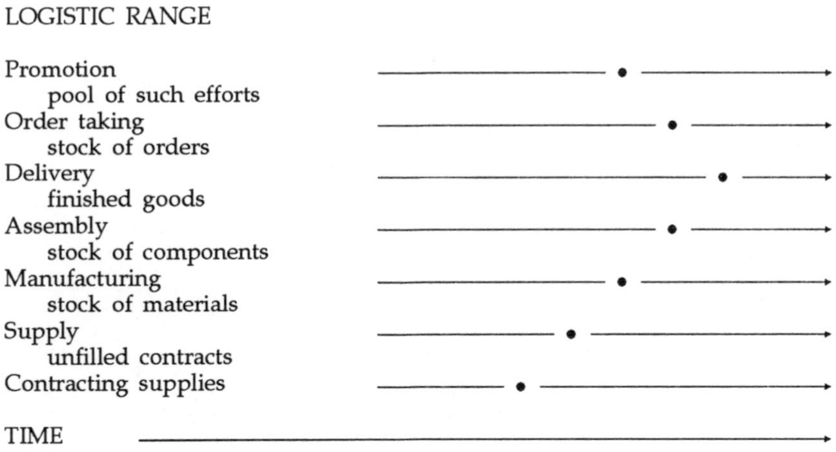

LOGISTIC RANGE

Promotion
    pool of such efforts
Order taking
    stock of orders
Delivery
    finished goods
Assembly
    stock of components
Manufacturing
    stock of materials
Supply
    unfilled contracts
Contracting supplies

TIME

Time, trade and logistics

Operations and stocks of the industrial firm move chronologically and logistically interconnected as shown in *figure 1*.

All operations run currently in time following a simple logic relation as to interdependence. Promotion is undertaken with the purpose of fortifying order taking. It is ahead in time and sequence as well. Manufacturing comes before assembly, that is the physical necessity. Note however, that especially on production, *figure 1* is an extremely simplified version.

Stocks interchange rhythmically with transactions as shown, and note that stocks comprise many levels in the commercial field of operations. So much for the conceptual frame; interest will now concentrate on essential numerical aspects.

Supplies account for nearly 60 percent of industrial costs, as appears from the information in *table 5*.

Results of business operations are evidently heavily influenced by purchase operations; companies would be expected to strive for much vigilance in that field for the same reason.

Industrial trade is characterized by orders and contracts; even apart from shipyards, the order books of industry usually range from 2-4 months of sales, as can be seen from *table 6*.

Table 5. Industrial accounts, 1985

	Million Kr.	Per cent
Operating income	260,888	100.0
Cost of goods sold	151,608	58.1
Wages and salaries	57,469	22.0
Other expenses	29,506	11.3
Depreciations	6,806	2.6
Result before financial items	15,496	5.9
Financial receipts	6,928	2.7
Financial expenses	7,343	2.8
Extraordinary items	223	0.1
Result before tax	15,304	5.9

Source: Industrial Accounts Statistics 1985, table 1. Danmarks Statistik, Nov. 1986.

Table 6. The duration of industrial order books (unfilled orders converted to number of months' sales)

The figure shows the largest and smallest number found among the monthly figures for the years 1984, '85, '86.

		Order books, measured in sales months	
ISIC	English title of category	Highest monthly figure	Lowest monthly figure
31	Food, beverages, tobacco	0.4	0.3
32	Textiles, wearing, leather	2.8	1.4
33	Wood products, furniture	2.6	1.5
34	Paper, printing, publishing	1.0	0.7
35	Chemicals (mainly petrol)	1.2	0.7
36	Non-metallic minerals	1.8	1.0
37	Basic metal industries	3.1	2.0
38	Fabricated metal	4.1	1.8
3841	- excl. shipbuilding		
2+3	Total, mining and manufacturing	1.9	1.3

Source: Monthly statistics of industrial sales and order books, table 8. Danmarks Statistik, December 1986.

For reliability, the figure shows the complete list of industry groups. Some show very low figures, below 1 month, but that should not cause confusion as to the statement on solid order books. The industries to appear with small figures are precisely those known for long-term contractual trading condition. Recall subscription arrangements within paper, printing and publishing, recall the tight distribution chains within petrol and recall the long-term arrangements for perishables within the food industry. In these branches, terms of notice replace ordering in advance. It is fully justified to state that stock of orders, in the broad sense of the word will only seldom be below 3 months' sales. The common textbook simplification of postulating two categories of industries, order producing or inventory producing, seems to be very misleading indeed. Note for later use that industry apparently is very well informed on sales volume and specifications for the next coming months.

Information on inventory holding is not very comprehensive in public statistics. They are end-of-the-year figures only, and distinguish among finished products and other stocks en bloc only. The interesting aspect is duration of stocks, for which *table 7* shows the reliable information available.

Table 7. The duration of industrial stocks

Sales of own products	255,703 million kr. the year
do.	21,309 million kr. monthly average
Stock of own products	22,491 million kr. opening
Duration of stocks	1,1 month of average sales
Raw materials, consumables and work in progress:	
Purchases	143,232 million kr. the year
Stock	16,110 million kr. opening
do.	17,636 million kr. closing
Consumption	141,706 million kr. the year
do.	11,809 million kr. monthly average
Duration of opening stock:	1,4 month of average consumption

Source: Industrial accounts statistics 1985, table 10. Danmarks Statistik, November 1986.

At the opening of the year, stocks of finished goods could last 1,1 month of average sales, the total of raw materials, consumables and work-in-progress 1,4 month of average consumption.

Note for later use that these figures are significantly below the duration of order books.

These are the few facts of industrial time and trade to be called upon for confrontation with the contents of OR/MS formulae.

Industry generally trades long-term or by order books; such procedure is not restricted to shipyards, but is simply common industrial practice. Order books are probably found on either side of the logistic range, but Danish statistics may not be sufficient here, as supplies of raw materials to a large degree arrive from abroad.

Order trading of the observed average duration and the observed variation in branches and seasons is the single most important fact that OR/MS seems to have bypassed in its conception of industrial life—to play an important role in the explanation to follow.

Formulae

Extracts

In this contribution to the explanation of OR/MS weaknesses special interest will be on aggregate planning and forecasting. Besides being a large subject in the discipline, as previously shown in *table 1*, aggregate planning constitutes the ideological and computational basis for the whole set of models. Inventory models and lot-sizing operate within the framework set by aggregate planning—to be further outlined in the section on consistency.

The case of aggregate planning is to be found in central and comprehensive models from each of the four source documents.

Buffa, after inspection of the methods of Linear Decision Rule, Management Coefficient Model, Parametric Production Planning and the Search Decision Rule summarizes in a 'generalized linear optimization model', which is taken as the typical version of what OR/MS has to offer in that edition (p. 312). To Hax & Candea, the text culminates in the Hierarchical Production Planning for a two-state system, the specification of which accordingly is taken as representative of what OR/MS stands for in that book (p. 429). Johnson & Montgomery seem to present their aggregate solution for industrial planning under the headline of multistage model, shown in various editions, from which one is chosen to substantiate their representation of what OR/MS can contribute in the field of aggregate planning (p. 259). Finally, in the book of Silver & Petersson, the authors recommend an algorithm of A.H. Land when a 'medium-range aggregate production planning' problem has to be solved. It is obviously their choice as to how OR/MS should be selected

(p. 553). These four models are used as basic representatives of the way in which OR/MS presents itself to the common educational scene.

One of the consented traits is the segregation of problem formulation in objective functions and a set of constraints. The examination of the texts will follow that line, objective functions for all four models to be examined concurrently and constraints to be taken as another connected subject for all four models.

This structure of formulae obviously leaves the question of which variables to place as constraints, which to place as variables with cost prices, and which perhaps to place both sides—and at what horizon. OR/MS seems to have adapted implicit standards here, but they could be less obvious in practice. I shall return to that aspect later on. So far observations are carried out within the structure of the discipline itself.

The extract of textbooks will, besides formulae, call attention to a topic that is never given specific chapters: Computation or rather computability. In explaining why OR/MS did fail empirically one cannot avoid observing the persistent information that—unfortunately—the methods and algorithms so carefully elaborated, are not suited for real-world problems. The obstacle commonly put forward is computational inability to handle larger amounts of data. Such information cannot be ignored in the explanation sought; it is highly relevant and will receive special attention in this text.

Objectives

The full contents of the four objective functions appear in *table 8* for a more careful inspection.

Firstly, optimization is brought about by minimizing a set of costs, demand accordingly being placed among constraints; this is common procedure. The mode of formulation is a set of Sigmas with nearly uniform notation as to sub- and topscript.

Everybody declares one common horizon T, segregated in intervals denoted t; that seems the first and consented specification. It allows for interval-planning, the typical aim of which is to balance a few sorts of costs over the season. Johnson & Montgomery and Hax & Candea, with subscript i specifies for either logistic stages or product types; these are not specified by Buffa, but by Silver & Petersson with a slightly different notation as to subscripts. The second part of Hax's expression rather duplicates the first part. K signifies parts, from which I are produced with a fixed and common lead time L. T, t and L—as presented here—is a valid representation on the concepts of time applied in OR/MS; an important characteristic to be pointed at later.

Table 8. Objective functions

Buffa (p. 312): Minimize

$$Z = \sum_{t=1}^{T} (c_t X_t + 1_t W_t + 1_t 0_t + h_t I_t^+ + \pi_t I_t^- + e_t w_t^+ + e_t w_t^-)$$

Silver & Peterson (p. 553):

$$\text{Min } C_{TOT} = \sum_{i=1}^{T} \sum_{j=1}^{k} \sum_{t=1}^{T} C_{ijt} \, p_{ijt} + \sum_{t=1}^{T} I_t vr_t$$

Johnson & Montgomery (p. 259): Minimize

$$Z = \sum_{t=1}^{T} \sum_{t=1}^{2} [c_{it} X_{it} + c_{it} Y_{it} + h_{it} I_{it}]$$

Hax & Candea (p. 432): problem P', minimize

$$\sum_{t=1}^{T} \sum_{i=1}^{I} (h_{it} I_{it} + r_t R_{it} + o_t O_{it}) + \sum_{t=1}^{T-L} \sum_{k=1}^{K} (\dot{h}_{kt} \dot{I}_{kt} + \dot{r}_{kt} \dot{R}_{kt} + \dot{o}_{kt} \dot{O}_{kt})$$

The rest of the functions are similarly alike, each term holding two factors, a unit consumption standard and a factor price, all specified according to the subscript. Notion and naming is almost stereotype, the list given in *table 9* is a complete enumeration with full text to evade elaborate notational listing for all four formulae.

The interest obviously is on balancing labour cost and inventory carrying; raw materials are either omitted or included, regarded as time independent and without constraints. The concept of cost is extraordinary simple—unit variable—and the costs are just there, ready for use in the specification needed.

This is the general criterion for decision of OR/MS aggregate planning, no more, no less. For later use in the text, special attention is directed at the single horizon, the omission of rawmaterials and components, the final-product focus and the simplicity of the cost concept.

Constraints

The constraints of the models are equally subscripted and similar, to be shown by reference to *table 10*. Expressions can be very sophisticated, but it is difficult to identify a logic of more than two elements.

Table 9. Cost types in OR/MS objective functions

	Term number in equation			
Cost type	Buffa p. 312	S&P p. 553	J&M p. 259	Hax p. 432
Regular hours	2		1	2
Overtime hours	3		2	3
Production cost unspecified	1	1		
Inventory carrying	4	2	3	1
Backorder	5			
Level decrease/increase	6,7			
Duplication of terms				4,5,6
Total number of terms	7	2	3	6

Table 10. Logic of OR/MS constraints

	Constraints no.:			
Type of logic	Buffa	S&P	J&M	Hax
End stock = beginning stock + production - demand	1,2	3,4	1,2	1,4
Consumption ≤ Capacity	3,4	1,2	3,4	2,3
(duplication by Hax)				4
Total number of constraints	4	4	4	4

The role of constraints is to secure that smoothing over the t-period season can proceed without loss of logic as to stocks, capacity, production and demand. Shadow prices of the dual solution apparently are not in the focus of the texts selected, but the logic involved permits such calculations, of course, as to demand and capacities.

These are the constraints found in the central expressions for aggregate planning in the top-four textbooks of OR/MS. Note for explanatory reasons some significant characteristics. Capacity constraints are on working hours of two sorts, not on plant, machinery, storeroom or items from outside supply; Silver & Petersson is an exception, defining only a general term of capacity and one joint production cost per unit: P_{ijt}. Production, stocks and demand are on finished products. Hax & Candea includes one previous part level, but that is all. Logistically OR/MS operates within a very narrow share of any realistic range.

Consistency

Within the frames of reference selected OR/MS appears a very consistent system.

The methods for prognostication of sales: Time-series analysis of past figures (trend, season, random) correspond neatly to the division of labour among aggregate planning and inventory /operations planning: Trend and season in aggregate planning for balancing stock and overtime, random variations to be taken care of in order point systems, which are simply designed for such a job.

By concentrating production planning on finished products, the necessary close correspondence between sales and production is secured. Proper production planning takes place within the chosen program. Optimal production, item by item, is secured by lot-sizing techniques, with due consideration of the inevitable randomness in demand.

The system is conceptually watertight and ready for service to industry. Unfortunately, the desired integration of methods, which will bring about full optimization is often restricted by comptational problems, to be reported of in the textbooks as well.

Computability

Textbooks will present persistent and nearly identical information on non-computability for realistic numbers of figures. The subject is never the main topic in these books, and some effort is needed to identify the information from throughout the texts. The intensiveness found is essential to the influence one can expect from the matter.

Already in 1974, Johnson & Montgomery had to state the inapplicability of large parts of their model for practical purposes. Inventory models can handle but single-item situation (p. 226).

Aggregate planning models cannot operate multiple-item and capacity-constraints simultaneously in the same algorithm for anything but very small problems (p. 248). No efficient exact solution procedures are known for the n-job, n-machine scheduling problem (p. 338). Johnson & Montgomery could still in 1974 obtain some confidence for the viewpoint that progress in programming software, size, and speed of computers would remove such difficulties. They prevail, however, in spite of the unquestionable progress in these matters.

Silver & Petersson reported in 1979 on such difficulties, sporadically (p. 307, p. 328) and terminating no less than 350 pages on inventory models by a summary stating that:

> With this chapter, we have dealt with the difficult multiechelon situation in which there is a dependency of demand among s.k.v. Exact analyses, particularly in the case of probalistic demand, quickly becomes intractable (p. 494).

Turning to production context in the remaining chapters, the prospect is still not encouraging:

> The sparse number of applications in this area is therefore in large part the result of two related reasons ...more and more complex models, which is not easy to adapt to changing real world situations... the manager is too often isolated from the process of achieving a 'solution'. (p. 564).

Hax & Candea bring the survey of OR/MS up to 1984: The difficulties reported in previous texts have not disappeared. On at least 10 points in the text non-applicability is reported of: On aggregate planning (p. 88, p. 101), on capacitated lot-size models (p. 96), on models with production change costs (p. 103), on multistage production planning (p. 238), on inventory control models (p. 239), on operations scheduling (p. 262, p. 322).

The topic is not sporadically treated by Hax and Candea. On the contrary, it usually appears as systematic closing note to larger sections of the text. The book actually provides computational verification for non-computability, even for modest numbers of data. The case showing that after 40 hours' machine time the majority of jobs had not yet been able to terminate, is a most convincing evidence of computational difficulties (p. 423).

Returning to the main point—explanation—it seems to be within the common sense of most people to expect that persistent and identical information on non-practicability could cause interest in any disciplin to fade away. It is certainly most disappointing to terminate a reading effort of 600 pages by being informed that hardly anybody use these methods.

Detachments

Explicitness

Specification of OR/MS' detachment from reality will be within preceding extracts of reality and texts.

To be accurate, one has to stick to the exact contents of phrases and formulae. What might be implicit to the author or what it could be extended to by some kind lecturer has no sense here. The manuscripts will have to be taken at face value.

Even then some problems of interpretation remains, especially on texts whose method is to present and finish a straightforward method while leaving, but actually mentioning, a lot of practical problems. Hax & Candea write (p. 433):

> To simplify the formulations of problem P, we have intentionally omitted planned backorders, hiring and firing, lost sales, and subcontracting. If needed, these can easily be incorporated.

How is such a sentence to be interpreted? Nobody can maintain that the authors did not mention the topics, it is even done in a self-assured and convincing way. To persist in asking for solutions would appear pedantic, even somewhat stupid; one should really be able to realize that and listen to the lecture given.

However, it has to be insisted that the authors did nothing byt state their intention not to involve such problems in the solution found. What the implications may be, is simply not cleared up. So, taken at the words, such delimitations in the texts are of minor interest. Interpretation will stick to factual handling and will observe what is actually incorporated.

Scope

It has to be stated that OR/MS by and large leaves out sales and purchase. The term demand is preferred and treatment is restricted to forecast of time series. Order books have no role to play, and the logistic range on top of *figure 1* is absent.

Nobody will seriously believe that business ignores such information in estimating sales. As to purchase, the only advice given might be in inventory models, aggregate planning is on production alone.

The critical point is the negligence of timing and the ordering delay. It may well be that production defines consumption and perhaps—as a derivative—deliveries needed, but that does not define contracting and the commercial commitments explicitly. Scope is inrealistically narrow in OR/MS, simply leaving out large parts of actual business operations.

Levels

As to production, the absolute main interest of OR/MS, it has to be observed that multilevel is not the favoured view. Planning is restricted to finished products or the blunt anonymous isolated item to be lot-sized or stored.

It could be objected of course that the consumption standards include everything and that predecessor levels easily can be derived. Besides, it should not be ignored that Hax introduces a parts level in his HPP-system (p. 430).

To insist on the unrealistic treatment of levels it has to be observed that programs have not direct engagement in the planning of supplies and previous manufacturing levels.

There is no direct explicit answer to the question of when to initiate inside and outside ordering.

Stockholding is presumed to contain finished products only; neither subscripts nor cost concepts allow for stocking semifinished products, another highly unrealistic attitude in seasonal balancing.

Note, that it is not postulated that the authors do not recognize these aspects of production. I only point to the fact that they cannot be found to play a notable role in the formulation of problems published. That is what matters to the reader, who is left alone, once again, with large practical tasks to be accomplished.

Costs

As can be seen from the objective functions (*table 8*), the concept of costs is straightforward and simple in OR/MS. It is generally 'unit-variable': Accurate and dynamic, specified on periods (t) and finished goods (x). The spectrum of cost types is quite small, tailored to the decision perspective used: Normal hours, overtime, stockholding, lot- or ordercharge. Raw materials are normally without interest, either omitted or just included, having no significant role to play.

28

The cost figures are just there—ready for use, an implicitness posing a risk for misinterpretation. It is probably fair to state, however, that they should be taken as some sort of user-cost in the accounting sense.

Costs are decisive for the programs chosen, but that foundation appears somewhat questionable. Firstly, the informed reader cannot help some astonishment at the phlegm shown by OR/MS to decades of cost theory. The simple unit-variable notion seems somewhat out of step with what is lectured elsewhere.

Even if such objections could be cleared away be reference to structure and subscripts in objective functions, it has to be maintained that costs are not just there to be supplied by some accounting department. Elaborate preparations may be necessary and doubt could soon arrive as to the realism of figures. At any rate, the relation of costs to factor market prices is obscure and underdefined. The prices to obtain by the firm in factor markets could possibly be dependent on the volume contracted. As to stockholding and order-charge the accounting attitude seems outright false; some 'marginal' or 'opportunity' concept appears much more realistic.

The silence of OR/MS on a subject that deserves explicit treatment leaves the discipline quite vulnerable.

Time

The last group of characteristics to be focused on is time, represented by four concepts: Horizon, interval, leadtime and frequency.

As has already been stated, OR/MS is stereotype here: One common horizon T, divided in t intervals, equal to all commitments. Leadtime is constant, equal to all products, aggregate, and measured in a number of t's. Frequency is almost implicit, per month or not mentioned at all—as required, may be.

The postulate on lack of realism takes its starting point in leadtime, which is either constant aggregate or equal. It has previously been stated, by reference to public statistics, (table 6) that the duration of order books is different to different types of industry and dependent on season and fluctuations of the markets as well. As a consequence, leadtime to the industrial firm would probably appear approximately as shown in figure 2.

Different terms and order book durations will have to be expected in different factor markets. The shorter lead-times can be found in production, but it is clearly unrealistic to imagine one aggregate lead-time. Recall the contents of table 6 and it is evident that business has excellent opportunities for flexibility. The notion of one common horizon for all commitments is clearly

Figure 2. Terms and lead-time

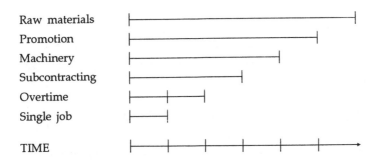

Commitments

out of consonance with realities. No businessman will ever commit his company further ahead than necessary. Business will operate different horizons for different commitments and need different intervals and frequencies for the same reason. The implicitness of time in OR/MS is a most serious detachment from realities.

To conclude

These are the four main characteristics of OR/MS to which I want to call attention in my search for the explanation: Detachments from realities as to scope, levels, costs and time.

Note that I do not postulate that OR/MS cannot handle purchase, levels, costs and lead-time appropriately. I am fully aware of the flexibility of mathematical method. I just state that the reader of predominant and recent textbooks has no way to know. Large administrative duties in industry are simply left out, and the texts cannot report on application for those methods described.

Textbooks could have certain educational duties, which might allow for some detachments from realities; a fair procedure of investigation accordingly requires observations elsewhere, in periodicals and conference papers to keep up to date.

As to periodicals, it has previously been found that aid is sparse which leaves papers from one of those events, where prominent representatives of the discipline meet to exchange views.

30

THE ESCAPISM OF OPERATIONS RESEARCH

Conference paper

Observation and Interpretation

The Mannheim Workshop on 'Multi-stage Production Planning and Inventory Control' took place in October 1985.

> During two days 40 specialists from 14 nations discussed 11 papers which were presented by research workers from many of the most active centers of production planning and inventory control all over the world.

With these words, the editorial committee presents the congress, the complete list of papers to be shown in *table 11*.

These are the papers to be examined as regards their attitude to the chosen characteristics: Scope, level, cost, and time. The aim of the text is not to evaluate these papers, but to make observations according to the objective previously stated: To explain the lack of practical application of OR/MS. Textbook extracts have served to specify the characteristics to look for and the review will be a target-oriented observation to see, whether those detachments from realities found in textbooks reappear in conference papers.

A short, but complete review of all papers is intended, and I shall follow the grouping selected by the editorial committee, according to whom, the first two groups are on modelling alone. I shall proceed immediately to the inspection announced, paper by paper.

Models

Paper no. 1 (Graves et al) allocates an aggregated safety stock on two levels. As to scope, selling takes the character of mean demand and standard deviation per item (p. 27); sufficient raw material is available (p. 29). The announced two-stage production reduces to considering a case, where each item on the first level will result in one unique item on the next level; by multi-item is meant about 30 numbers. No cost or factor price is applied, the model operates on 'filling rate' of inventories. As to time, each level has a fixed lead time equal to all items (p. 27) and the simulation run assumes a time unit of one month and a demand forecast 12 month' ahead for each item. The test run compares inventory filling for two different models.

As can be seen, the simplification of textbooks' scope, level, cost, and time has by no means been altered and it is very difficult to find real world significance of the test arrangement.

Paper no. 2 (Joensson/Silver) is a 5-page story on allocation of inventories for a two-echelon system with constant average demand, pure distri-

Table 11. Conference papers—Mannheim

bution with no production or supply mentioned, a fixed horizon, a cycle of a predetermined fixed number of periods, and no lead-time mentioned. A short-story, to be short, of principal character.

Paper no. 3 (Luyten) applies the Markovian Decision Process on a extremely reduced system (p. 60) which allows full calculation of 'optimal inventory policy'. Correspondence to real world situation is hardly intended and difficult to find. Scope certainly does not include supplies, and demand is for only one type of item that can be sold in numbers of either 0, 1 or 2 pieces with known and constant probabilities in each period equal for two retailers. A few combinations of fixed setup-, holding-, shortage- and unit costs are chosen for calculation; familiar concepts, but an extremely reduced number of figures for computational reasons. Lead time is a known constant, and horizon T is divided in periods, the familiar set again.

Paper no. 4 (Gelders et al.) introduces itself as follows (p. 93):

> The multi item single level capacitated dynamic lotsizing problem consists of scheduling N items over a horizon of T periods. Demands are given and should be satisfied without backlogging. The objective is to minimize the sum of set up costs and inventory holding costs over the horizon, subject to a single constraint on total capacity in each period.'

An algorithm is presented for solution. As can be seen the specification as to scope, level, cost and time is identical to textbook formulae and the authors conclude (p. 106) on immense computational difficulties as well.

The objective of paper no. 5 (Axsaeter/Nuttle) is

> to generate a production/purchase plan to minimize total set up plus inventory carrying cost over a T-period horizon. End item demand in each period is known, but may vary from period to period, cost parameters are constant over time, initial inventories are zero for all items, and lead times are constant so that they may be ignored ... one unit of any item requires one unit of its immediate predecessor item.'

Textbook delimitations seem fully repeated here.

Paper no. 6 (Rosling) develops an exact algorithm for a single-item lotsizing problem. The interest is on applying Bender's algoritm, not on scope, levels, time or cost. Common theoretical notation is applied.

Paper no. 7 (Muckstadt) is remarkable from the point of view of this survey, as it proclaims to focus on (p. 132):

> the time between external procurements and between movement of stock from stage to stage for each component in a multistage assembly system ...

John Muckstadt's aim is, however, restricted to

> develop a model and an algorithm that can be used to establish consistent and realistic economic delivery intervals for each component

while recognizing the presence of some of the capacity constraints mentioned earlier. (Receiving dock capacity and storage area capacity).

The economic delivery interval is seen as a substitute to lot-sizing, which unfortunately reduces the problem considerably. Demand is constant and continuous, and ordering, as distinguised from delivery, remains an opening note. As to levels, 7 store areas are defined, but the focus of interest is on economic delivery as a lot-sizing substitute. The model operates within a fixed and abstract horizon with no calender time intervals, lead time is not considered at all.

Paper no. 8 (Heinrich/Schneeweiss) on multi-stage lot-sizing for general production system brings back on familiar ground. Scope does not include buying and selling, demand is known or normally distributed, and cost comprises fixed charge cost and linear holding alone. As to levels, the paper clearly expands to five chosen multi-stage structures. Horizon is finite over t periods, lead time can be ignored, being constant. Simulation runs alter cycle times in testing the effectiveness of a series of lot-size methods.

Paper no. 8 terminates the group of papers, for which the editor declares that validation should respect the plain character of models. I have intended no validation at all, just observations as announced. Conclusion on the papers will be joint, including the last group, which carries a promise on application in the editorial naming.

Applications

The three last papers are announced as practical applications, quite a bold statement, as none of the papers can pride themselves on describing OR/MS systems in steady service. They are all preliminary attempt to try application on real word problems, and the reports given hardly makes it possible for the outside observer to evaluate the chance of sucess.

Paper no. 9 (Donselaar, Winjgaard) deals with a 6 level system (p. 183) of Philips, in order to seek reduction of stockholding. The authors reduce the scope of logistics to a two-level system for aggregate production and presume stochastic lead-time, known standard deviation on demand forecast, and infinite capacity. It is not altogether convincing, how this reduction fits with the original problem even when it makes convincing simulation runs. Textbook-notions are fully realized in the delimitated version.

In paper no. 10, Stadtler sets out by describing the company of a German food manufacturer: A plant of 7 labour-interdependent departments, 5 processing lines and 9 packaging lines, a chain with no possibility for stocking as products are perishables. The number of items runs to the hundreds and set-up-times are sequence dependent. Within these frames, the author looks for improvement of the planning system. The choice is the Hax/Bitran model: Types-families-items, and some simplifying assumptions are introduced (p. 201)! The number of logistic levels are reduced to two, demand and a chosen limiting production stage; set-up times are assumed not—sequence dependent. The model chosen then balances stockholding and set-up cost (p. 209), in strict accordance with Hax/Bitran, but astonishing compared to the needs and conditions of the company previously described. The point of Stadtler is that the Hax/Bitran idea of forecasting on the product type level is not feasible for effective lot-sizing; forecasts should be on more accurate levels, family or item.

As can be seen, scope and levels of the firm are reduced as to fit textbook standards, the concept of cost apparently too. Lot-sizing takes place within a fixed and common horizon (p. 211) and lead-time considerations do not appear. There is no evidence on practical application of the model.

The last paper from the conference (Guenther) is on the planning problems of a washing powder company, and Hax et al. is the favoured source of inspiration once again. Guenther shows an interesting attempt at widening scope, levels and time in order to handle procurement and manpower (p. 240) but soon falls back on familiar OR/MS ground. The set of concepts maneuvered in the modelling (p. 244) is the common one, set-up cost, holding cost, net-requirements etc.

Guenther defines three decision levels: Lot-sizing, item disaggregation and distribution. His method is to define each problem according to recognized LP viewpoints (p. 244, 248, 253) followed by reference to specified investigation by others, which consequently shows, that—due to numerical complexity—it is not solvable by that suggestion. Solutions are found in Guenther's own heuristics for lot-sizing, each described by 'structograms' operating on familiar cost concepts. As to scope, levels and time, familiar viewpoints are observed: Demand, one-level production, T and t.

Paper no 11 terminates the contribution of the Mannheim workshop to 'multi-stage production planning and inventory control'. It terminates the observations on OR/MS texts of this manuscript as well, to be concluded in combination with the textbook observations previously described.

OR/MS characteristics

The conclusion on the characteristics of literature can be unambigous: Textbooks and conference papers are much alike.

As to computational difficulties, no evidence is presented that could weaken the opinion of textbook authors. On the contrary, over and over again, conference papers confirm what has already been stated in that respect.

On the scope of planning, the conclusion can be plain: Neither textbooks nor conference papers recognize the mercantile functions of the firm. Relations to markets in sale and purchase—on as well prices as volumes—are obscure, underdefined or not specified at all.

As to levels, the general attitude in conference papers is to reduce even obviously multi-level problem to two-level—in the logistic sense of the word. Some lack of precision as to the meaning of level, stage or echelon seems observable. At least four different opinions seem presented: Logistics (Leyten), product-structure (Axaeter/Nuttle), the Hax' dimension of type-, family-item and finally a planning-procedure focus (Guenther). This survey has concentrated on the logistic aspect and a minor development from textbooks to congress papers seems observable. From one to two levels in lotsizing, but very restricted by the one-item throughput assumption and the lack of consideration for timing. It is hardly unfair to state that the finished-product or single-item view is still predominant and sufficient within OR/MS circles.

Costs still follow adapted ways, lot, charge and inventory-carrying in the user cost accounting way. None of the conference papers operate on opportunity cost, shadow prices or dual solution—consistently enough—the relation to factor markets being obscure.

Neither on time can notable differences be regarded as having much weight. The notion of 'decision window' which seems new is not carried forward as to influence models. The fixed and common T, t and L stand the unshakeable pattern.

As a final word: Neither textbooks nor conference papers are evaluated from any point of view, they are inspected in order to identify the state as to certain characteristics selected and declared in advance. I am well aware of the different modes of validation possible, but none are relevant here.

Much could be said in favour of the texts employed, much scepticism could be appropriate as well, from different points of view, but I have refrained from that. The intention at least, of the textual examination has been on observation alone, the purpose was to identify the elements of the explanation to follow.

CHAPTER 4

Consequences

Explanation

Having outlined the conditions of reality chosen and the observations found relevant as to literature, time has come to explain the weak empirical stand of OR/MS.

Investigations in reality and in literature would hopefully carry a strong element of objectivity, verification or falsification open to everyone. The combination for explanatory purpose is different, a plain subjective choice.

None the less, it is not just a haphazard affair, it implies at least some criteria that can be stated explicitly in advance; some of the opening grounds for choice of literature are recalled.

If proposed methods are found irrelevant when confronted to realities, there is a cause for explanation. If OR/MS is silent or highly abstract compared to the management jobs needed done, another cause for explanation arise. No discipline can expect its proposals to be attractive if the consonance to realities is obscure or lacking. It might even be doubtfull whether it deserves the name of science.

Three lines of thought are pursued for explanation, compatibility, competence and consistency, the main points of which are as follows.

Compatibility is on the meaning of the concepts employed in OR/MS. Even if they seem fair enough and well motivated, one by one, their combination could define an impossible situation. This is the first stumbling block, large enough perhaps, to reduce interest for further investigation on applicability.

The second line of thought is on competence or relevans of OR/MS texts. They do not appear persuasive—too many unanswered questions, too much silence on essential and demanding planning jobs.

The third and last line of thought challenges the intrinsic value of the central theory of OR/MS itself: Primary and dual solution, objective function and constraints. The theory seems to have only restricted generality, tied to conditions whose implications are never considered. If the conditions necessary for consistency are stated, the lack of realism is obvious. If they are relaxed for matters of adaptation, the theory appears even self-contra-dictory.

These three lines of thought would have to be supplemented by the difficulties of computation already treated.

Such are the four main points of explanation attempted. Conclusion will be joint, implying evaluation of the aggregate manuscript, to be delivered in the last chapter.

Compatibility

OR/MS promises an optimal aggregate program for a common horizon, clearly a most attractive perspective.

Even on the conceptual level such a promise is doubtful, as can be seen by comparing the very combinations of concepts.

The criterion of optimality is an abstract notion incompatible with a future horizon. Sales forecasts cannot avoid being uncertain and to select, not to say, follow a production program chosen from that criterion would most unlikely bring about achievements that could be called optimal.

It could be objected of course that OR/MS does not prevent the program from being altered when forecasts change, but that is not sufficient defense. Most commercial contracting has to be carried out on a longer term, where uncertainty cannot be disposed of. To commit the firm in such matters on the criterion of optimality in the strict and narrow OR/MS-sense would appear most irresponsible. A criterion of robustness or the more general concept of rationality found in the Decision Theory seems much more appropriate. For long term commitments considerations of 'averageness' appear much more in line with common sense than optimality.

Compatibility of concepts of course, depend on the meaning attached to the words employed. When OR/MS restricts the meaning of optimality to the selected mathematical expressions, optimality— in the general sense of the word—simply cannot be achieved. Optimum is a general word of value, however, and it remains very odd indeed to observe that solutions, obviously very narrow-minded, boast themselves of optimality. Real-life occurrences, on the other hand, can never be optimal, not for matters of reality, but simply as a consequence of a restricted meaning attached to a general word.

Common sense would state that sensible, or rational, or optimal behaviour is within absolute reach of any businessman, but he should clearly react more prudently to future commitment than OR/MS programs allow for.

Sticking to established combinations here, will probably tend to isolate OR/MS from business.

Competence

Business operations

Alongside the incompatibility of concepts, OR/MS seems to have difficulties in rendering answers to the questions of business even within areas for which it claims to bring solutions. Its general competence within the general field where it asserts to operate—Management of Operations—seems highly questionable. Take the prime operations of industry: Purchase, production and sale.

Purchase

The buying side of business operations can hardly postulate to be a main subject of OR/MS, even if it accounts for about 60 percent of costs, provides for market price information in calculations, and carries a major risk for business. Recall the long term conditions of industrial trade and observe the assistance offered by OR/MS: Either implicitly derived from aggregate planning or by means of inventory models.

Aggregate planning clearly aims at long term and seasonal adjustment, but focus is on production and very often on manpower requirements. Silence generally prevails on supplies of rawmaterials and components.

Derivation seems the only solution, but even here, texts are silent. As production figures are selected by the program, however, timephased by t's, requirements for supply can simply be derived by calculation. The problem appears trivial, theoretically anyway.

However, it should be recalled that the time phasing of aggregate production planning is on end-products solely and that lead-time, as applied, is always one single figure, intended to cover up for all production levels and purchase collectively. But different markets have different lead-times and lead-time of production depends on the time-horizon applied. Besides, market conditions in supply can hardly avoid pushing back on sales and production. The problems are not so trivial anyway and the reader gets no aid from OR/MS, the implicit solution pointed at, seems to carry great risks for unwise decisions. Implicitness could be reason enough for the reader to loose interest in the texts.

Turning to inventory models for purchase does not offer much assistance either, even if their vocabulary clearly operates on ordering, lead time, and supply. Serious drawbacks will have to be remembered, especially with reference to Orlicky. The conditions for use of the OR/MS spectrum of models for contineous demand, service-level, etc could hardly ever be expected to be found in the dependent demand of industrial supplies. No convincing circumstances can be found either, as to coping with long term contracting using these models. The main interest on balancing ordering cost per order and inventory holding costs indicates that focus is on delivery—which is shortsighted—not on trade, the long-term commitments.

Purchase really seems to be an underdefined subject in general accessible OR/MS-texts, a serious obstacle indeed to further interest in the discipline considering its importance for business.

Production

Lack of interest can certainly not be found when it comes to production, by far the largest OR/MS subject. Even then application seems lacking, the reason possibly being that the discipline cannot answer the questions actually posed in the world of realities. Neither aggregate planning nor inventory/lot-sizing offer sufficient guidance.

Aggregate planning takes the shape of a production program for end-products defined for all t's of the horizon T. The program chooses the mix preferable and balances production and inventories optimally over the season. Demand, manpower, and other required capacities, neatly specified by t's, are taken note of. Shadow prices rarely attract attention in the texts; the calculated program is the proven optimum, ready for execution.

Such a program could hardly be relevant for the nearest future, the one, for which order books already tie the firm. Programming production implies a freedom of action which on the average (*table 6*) does not seem to exist for the nearest 2-4 month. For that period the calculated program for end-product production can hardly be expected to be relevant.

No harm done, the program can be pushed ahead in time in order to select the optimal program for a future, which is yet not restricted by orders, already received. It may even be the right spot for focus of planning, to manage order taking in advance so as to steer sales towards the most favourable program. All that makes good sense in principle, but it seems to invalidate the very meaning of the OR/MS formulae, its raison d'être perhaps.

Essential for explanatory reasons is first and foremost that the program only under very rare circumstances can be expected to define an end-product production that would be realized. If lead-time in production is larger that

the period covered by order-books, the solution might be valid—in principle—but such a relation will hardly ever turn up. Recall that the program
is on end-products, i.e. on the final production level and inventory level
only. Pushing ahead will gradually reduce the very essence of the OR-
expression.

Demand-forecast is not the only element of conditions, whose uncertainty
increase with the length of horizon. Supply, prices, and lead-times of all
production factors, and manpower not the least. Nobody will deny that all
the factors should be weighed against one-another, but the very strict
expression of objective function and constraints seems somewhat out of consonance with a scene, where constraints gradually vanish and the price-
component of the objective function most likely will be influenced by the
program chosen. On the more strictly mathematical side, such a development
means difficulties with the duality principle as such, to which I shall return
in the next section.

Now turn to the exact result of the aggregate planning, the end-products.
Even if that program is found favourable, it is undeniable that the aggregate
plan delivers no direct answer as to what to produce on previous levels in
the nearest future. An answer might be found by derivation, but the process
is by and large undefined in OR/MS-texts, a silence of considerable
importance to non-application.

As regards aggregate planning, it must be maintained that it leaves management with nearly no answers at all of what to produce at level 'i' in
interval 't'; on the possible derivatives in previous levels: Stock and
purchase, silence still prevails.

To proceed in the explanation, now turn to the next device of OR/MS,
inventory/lot-sizing-models, which might do the job. The conditions usually
required here: That demand should be known or randomly distributed—trend and season disposed of by aggregate planning—seem to be
fully satisfied by exactly that orderbook, which made aggregate planning
questionable. Why then, the meager application reported?

These models generally operate on holding costs and fixed sequence-
independent order costs that are balanced in more or less sophisticated shape
over a known horizon. But if demand is certain and shipments to customers
secured by order books, inventories of end-products are very unlikely,
however, the point of balancing holding costs at all accordingly being quite
irrelevant. If shipments are secured, it is always favourable to increase lotsize
and nothing has to be stored.

Add to this the analysis of Orlicky according to whom the choice of lot-sizing model appeared rather irrelevant (p. 136). The general one-level models of lot-sizing are hardly fit for the dependent time-phased demand along industrial logistics. Results of models depend largely on horizon and planning-intervals chosen. As to selection of T and t, OR/MS offers no advice, as will be known.

The optimizing vocabulary seems to be somewhat out of consonance to the practical conditions and the planning jobs that need to be done. The lack of alertness to time, trade and logistics leaves production with many unanswered questions, probably too many to make the methods attractive. The answers actually delivered are on questions never asked.

Sale

The selling side of business can hardly be said to carry much weight in either OR/MS textbook or in conference papers. Textbooks furnish methods for forecasting time series as regards trend, season and randomness; conference papers regard demand as known, i.e. announced from outside.

A short note on the lack of precision as how to define sales in OR/MS cannot be avoided. The analysis of time series does not reveal, at what point in the selling process sales are defined: Ordering point, delivery or invoicing. The choice is decisive for planning purposes, it makes a difference of 2-4 month's lead-time, and it has to be stated again: OR/MS leaves many open questions and does not really seem to engage in business operations.

The modest position in textbooks and conference papers seems to conflict considerably however to the observations on periodicals (*table 4*) where market-research projects obviously take a strong position; they account for no less than 26 out of 97 applications reported of—to be compared to 1 on industry-planning. How could that correspond? Are textbooks becoming ab-solute here? The answer is probably the decoupling of time and dynamics in marketing-projects: Their task is to compare markets, products, distribution channels, promotion media, etc in order to find an optimal mix for some abstract unbound future period. No current business is implied.

In short, when time is out, OR/MS seems feasible, an explanation very consistent to the phlegm of the discipline as to the dynamic interconnec-tedness in business, difficult perhaps to correspond to the chosen name of Operations Research.

Consistency

OR/MS was found to be a consistent system in chapter 3, the division of labour among forecasting, aggregate, lot-sizing and inventory appearing most convincing. It was stated too that the consistency prevailed within the frames of reference selected.

At least some of these frames are made explicit here, in order to show that the generality claimed by OR/MS is within very narrow limits. Only very small deviations from consented assumptions will probably force the inner consistency to collapse.

What should be made explicit is that OR/MS does not handle and cannot handle operations of different horizons, and different leadtimes. In the end that implies that it cannot handle business operations at all, at least not in the shape known today. The very notion of primacy and duality, the combined set of objective function and constraints becomes open to doubt.

The combined reasoning of solution and dual solution runs as follows: The program chooses the optimal program under the given constraints. It calculates as dual solution the shadow prices of constraints. The more sophisticated interpretations will emphasize that before action is taken according to the prime solution, shadow prices should be compared to factor prices. If relations are favourable, constraints should be altered and the program rerun for improvement. Another consistent reasoning, which has to be reviewed however in the light of *figure 2* (page 29 above).

The time of decision is always zero and the firm has to make its commitments according to terms and lead-times in the various factor markets in which it operates. It implies on the other hand that as time zero is approached from right to left, the more is predetermined. The variety of terms and lead-times to be found in real life means as follows to objective functions and constraints: The more the point of decision is approached, the more the objective function is emptied for its content. Variables are continuously being converted to constraints, for which—according to the main idea of OR/MS—only opportunity costs are relevant. I presume everyone will agree that the cost figures to appear in the objective function could have only one source: The market commitments on rawmaterials, wages, etc.

A peculiar paradox seems to emerge then. As the need of cost functions increases in order to decide on production, the cost function is emptied. The establishment of shadow prices, which a transfer to constraints gives rise to, is of very little operational significance as the opportunity for supply has gone with passed terms and leadtimes.

Shadow prices are established for a period, for which they are irrelevant, and cost prices disappear or become irrelevant for the period for which they are intended to constitute the background for decision.

A combined solution is possible, formally at least, having the same factor of production represented in the objective function and as constraint as well. Mathematically it would cause no problem, as the objective function would apply a cost price and constraints operate the volume available. The solution found would probably be irrelevant for either of two reasons. If the shadow price is zero, the production factor is free, and the cost price of the objective function clearly misleading. If the shadow price is larger than the cost price but no supplementary supplies available for matters of passed lead-times, constraints are relevant, cost price thus being a misleading decision criterion.

For explanatory reasons: This is not just some subtle mathematical interpretation, but a simple straightforward observation. If the men are free, but not to be fired, the cost of using their time is zero and any job reasonable. Are they already making money for the firm you have to consider what is lost by transfer to other duties, irrespective of their actual wages. Any supervisor can see that, and programming solutions that cannot cope commitments of different leadtimes will appear unreasonable.

Within the area of different leadtimes, OR/MS apparently does not seem to be very fit; its area of validity seems to be beyond the widest term and lead-time, where freedom of commitment prevails. At least no formal inconsistencies pose difficulties then.

Still, a widening horizon implies obvious risks for ending up in the situation described by Winston in his analysis of the Duality Theory (p. 129): The price criterion of the objective function could become derivative of the very same program, which the objective function is intended to select. The price conditions for rawmaterials and components could hardly be expected to be independent of the volume traded.

Moving ahead in time does not seem to furnish OR/MS with a solid working field either. Inconsistency could easily result and application accordingly of poor value.

It seems necessary to terminate by stating that the expressions of OR/MS, as known in the texts referred to, straightaway assume that business commitments have no or common lead time. In view of market conditions, revealed from a host of sources, this is utmost unrealistic. The assumption seems difficult to loosen without seriously inflicting the central ideology of OR/MS.

CHAPTER 5

Evaluation and Odds

In summing up, it is customary to evaluate the platform of conclusion pointing especially to the weaker points.

Firstly, it should be remembered that the outset was a desire to seek for explation of a meager empirical record by means of more intensive inspection of OR/MS.

The postulates of Ackoff, Eilon and others have been further cleared by reference to reported investigations and inspection of periodicals. The platform for opinion has been enlarged here, which did not seem to weaken the points of the writers mentioned.

The characteristics of OR/MS had to be substantiated in order to allow for intensive inspection. To cover the full area of periodicals and book seemed both impossible and unnecessary for the purpose and likely impact of the ideas presented. Well-recommended and well-referenced books by the main debators of congresses and periodicals seemed sufficient for the purpose. To safeguard against the risk of obsolescence of books, inspection of the reports to a recent high-level congress has taken place. More books, periodicals and congress reports can of course easily be added for securing a more valid expression on the content of the discipline, but it should be pointed out that the contents already found reveal only minor dissimilarities.

To back the postulates on detachment from realities, reality has to be defined and verified. Definition is clearly open to doubt as to selection and omission of aspects, but a choice had to be made and the well-known weaknesses of the behavioural sciences as to lack of security on the 'everything else equal' condition is still involved here. On the other hand the components of reality referred to have been backed by official, publicly accessible Danish statistics on industry. No efforts to inspect statistics from other countries have been carried out, but might possibly be done elsewhere, if interest in the views of the article makes it worthwhile. The information used is by no means sophisticated.

The detachments from reality include computability and the more specific properties of OR/MS. As to computability, sustained and identical statements on lack of practicability can be identified in as well textbooks as conference reports. As to the properties of OR/MS, my postulates on lack of realism must obviously be subjective at the outset. Interpretation of literature has to be carried out in order to justify these postulates. Textbooks are used for the first inspection, later backed by conference paper's inspection. Detachments from reality comprise mainly time and trade, to be inspected by investigating scope, levels, costs and time of OR/MS texts. Conference contributions seemed astonishingly faithfull to textbook views.

The explanation aimed at combines the information presented on realities and the OR/MS discipline. It is found incompatible, unable to render the answers needed by business and even conceptually inconsistent, when time and trade is introduced.

The difficulties encountered in my view seem to present very serious difficulty to the profession. It cannot be doubted that trade and time can conceptually be incorporated—the technique of mathematics is extremely flexible, but it cannot avoid weighing on the computational situation, which already seems serious enough.

Following the views of Ackoff and Eilon the most serious mistake of those advocating the discipline is probable the distance selected to the empirical principle.

Professor Schneeweiss in his introduction to the Mannheim congress explicitly defined a two-step validation method (p. 2) which permits abstraction from the empirical validation seeking rescue in controlled simulation runs on computers.

A discipline, which isolates itself from the test of realities by such means, takes great risks for getting out of contact to the empirical field. The educational appeal, which consistent and proved systems seem to carry, cannot in the long run survive a serious and persistent lack of consonance with the real world.

References

Ackoff, R.L. 1979. The Future of Operational Research is Past, *J. Opl. Res. Soc.* Vol. 30,

Axaeter, S., Schneeweiss, Ch., and Silver, E. 1985. *Multi-stage Production Planning and Inventory Control.* Lecture Notes in Economics and Mathematical Systems no. 266, Berlin.

Buffa, Elwood S. 1983. *Modern Production/Operations Management*, New York.

Eilon, Samuel. 1985. *Management Assertions & Aversions*, Oxford.

Eiselt, H.A., Eiselt, G.R. and Sandblom, C.L. 1986. A Survey of Operations Research in Canadian Companies, *INFOR*, Vol. 24.

Hax, Arnoldo C. and Candea, Dan. 1984. *Production and Inventory Management*, New Jersey.

Hoque, Jack T. and Watson, Hugh J. 1986. *Current Practices in the Development of Decision Support Systems* in Spraque and Watson: Decision Support Systems, New Jersey.

Interfaces 1984—1985—1986

Johnson, L.A. and Montgomery, D.C. 1973. *Operations Research in Production Planning, Scheduling and Inventory Control*, New York.

Lilien, Gary L. 1987. MS/OR: A Mid-life Crisis, *Interfaces* Vol. 17.

Lockett, G. 8—1985. Application of Mathematical Programming: *Management Science.*

Orlicky, Joseph. 1975 *Material Requirements Planning*, New York.

Silver, E.A. and Peterson, Rein. 1985. *Decision Systems for Inventory Management*, New York.

Winston, Gordon C, 1982. *The Timing of Economic Activities*, Cambridge.